Thailand Fun Facts Picture Book for Kids

An Educational City Travel Photography Photobook About History, Places with Everything You Need to Know About the Country for Children & Teens

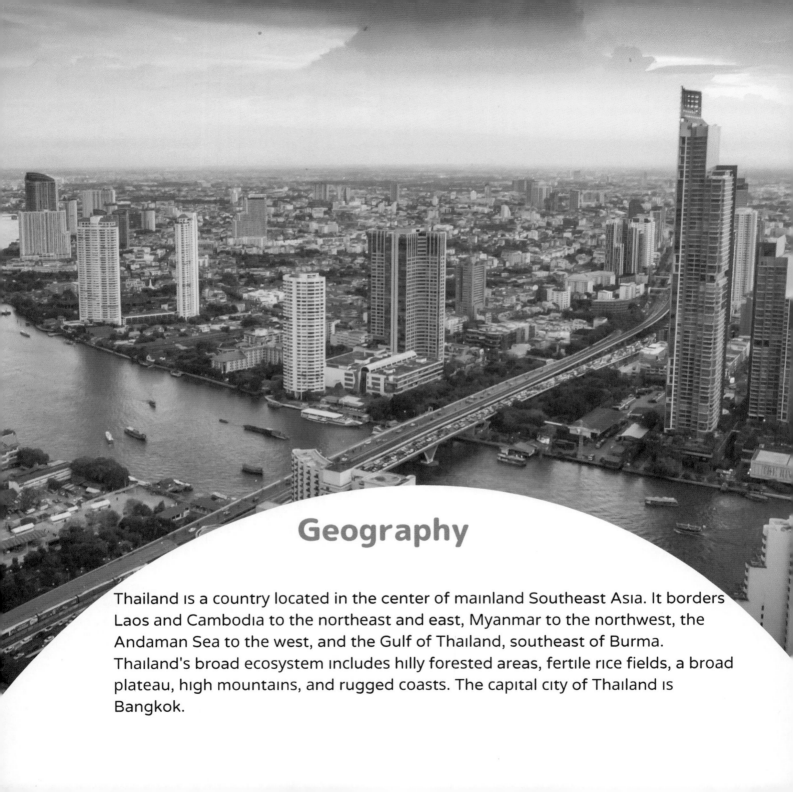

Geography

Thailand is a country located in the center of mainland Southeast Asia. It borders Laos and Cambodia to the northeast and east, Myanmar to the northwest, the Andaman Sea to the west, and the Gulf of Thailand, southeast of Burma. Thailand's broad ecosystem includes hilly forested areas, fertile rice fields, a broad plateau, high mountains, and rugged coasts. The capital city of Thailand is Bangkok.

History

The first settlement was built in the hillsides of Thailand around 2000 B.C. The first kingdom of Thailand Sukhothai was founded by King Sri Indraditya in 1238. After the Sukhothai era, new kingdoms such as Ayutthaya, Rattanakosin, and Thonburi arose, and each era has its historical events and exciting cultural changes.

The Rattanakosin period started when King Yot Fa founded the Chakri dynasty and chose Bangkok as the capital. Western countries invaded, but the king reached an agreement with them to preserve the country. Thailand changed from the monarchy system to the democratic system that they used till the present in 1932. It was renamed Thailand, meaning land of the free, in 1939.

Did you know

Thailand was never colonized by a European country and it's the only southeast Asian country to achieve that feat.

Climate

Thailand has a tropical climate with three unique seasons. Hot season(March-mid-May), rainy season(mid-May-October), and the dry and hot season(Nov-Feb). The cool season happens most in the north and inland areas. The south and the coastal area are usually hot, even in winter.

People

The people of Thailand are known as Thais, and it can refer to both Thailand citizens and ethnic Thais. Most of the population are ethnic Thai(about 75%) and ethnic Chinese(14%). Other ethnic groups include Malay-speaking Muslims, Khmers, Kui, Karen, Pakistanis, and Indians.

Many Thais are Buddhist. The national language is Thai, and there are more than 70 other languages in the country.

Residents in each region of Thailand have particular characteristics and looks that describe them because of the difference in geography and environment. Northern Thais seem calm, gentle, and speak softly. Southern Thais are fast in their speech and decision-making. Boys usually start military training in 9th grade.

Thailand fun facts

Most Thais Have A Nickname

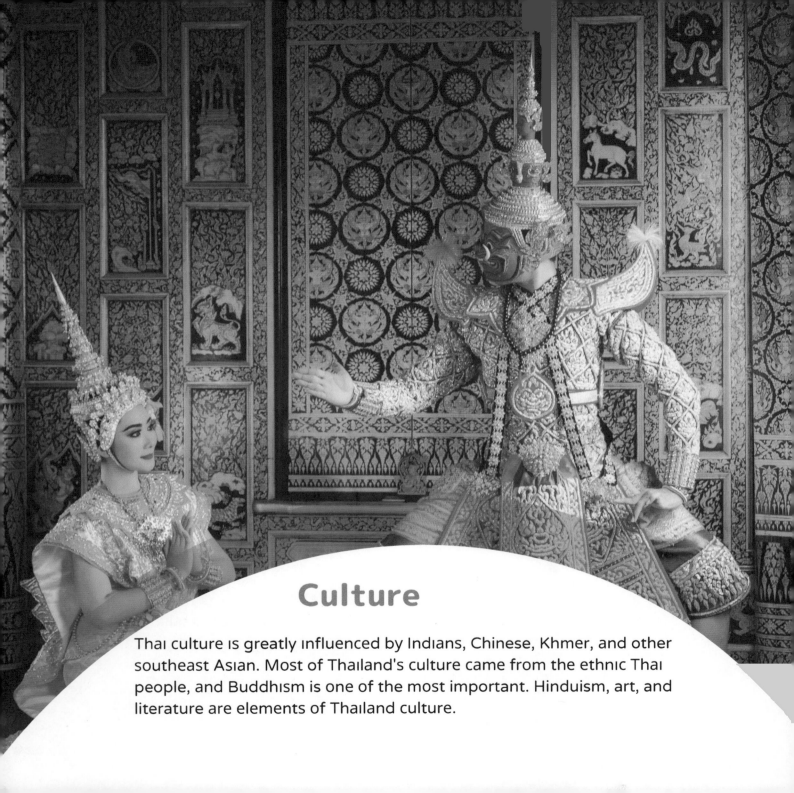

Culture

Thai culture is greatly influenced by Indians, Chinese, Khmer, and other southeast Asian. Most of Thailand's culture came from the ethnic Thai people, and Buddhism is one of the most important. Hinduism, art, and literature are elements of Thailand culture.

THAILAND FUN FACTS

The Thai Language Has 76 Letters

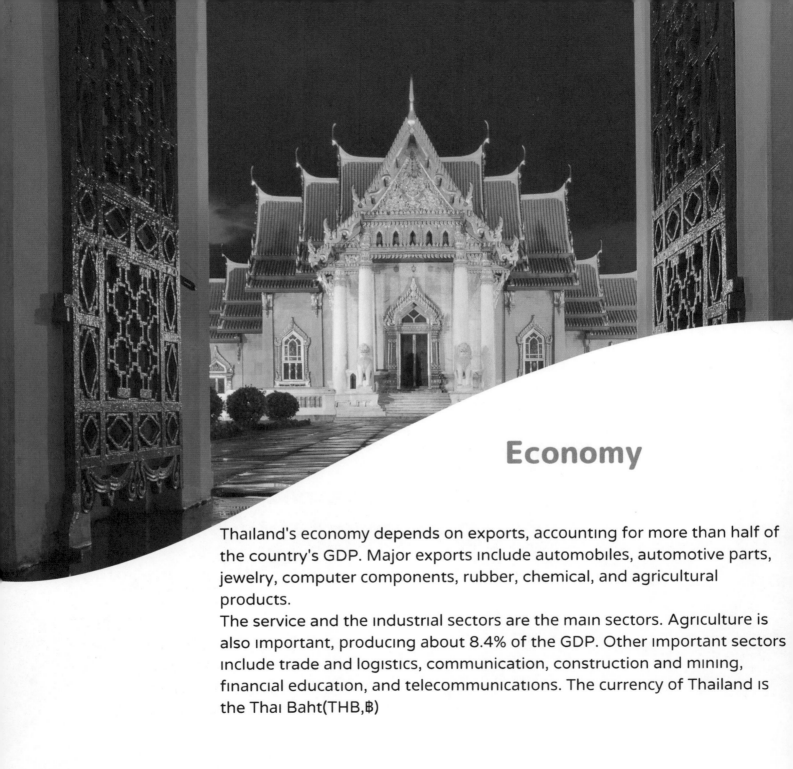

Economy

Thailand's economy depends on exports, accounting for more than half of the country's GDP. Major exports include automobiles, automotive parts, jewelry, computer components, rubber, chemical, and agricultural products.

The service and the industrial sectors are the main sectors. Agriculture is also important, producing about 8.4% of the GDP. Other important sectors include trade and logistics, communication, construction and mining, financial education, and telecommunications. The currency of Thailand is the Thai Baht(THB,฿)

Public Holidays

Business and government offices in Thailand are closed for public holidays, but tourist attractions and shops might remain open. Below are the most important national holidays in Thailand.

New Year's Day- Jan 1st
Makha Bucha- Mar 4
Chakri Day- April 8
Songkran(Thai New Year)- April 13-15.
Labor Day- May 1st
Coronation Day- May 5
Visakha Bucha- Jun 1st
Asalha Bucha- July 30
Buddhist Lent-July 31st
Queen's Birthday- Aug 12
Chulalongkorn's Memorial Day- Oct 23
King's Birthday- Dec 5
Constitution Day- Dec 10
New Years' Eve- Dec 31

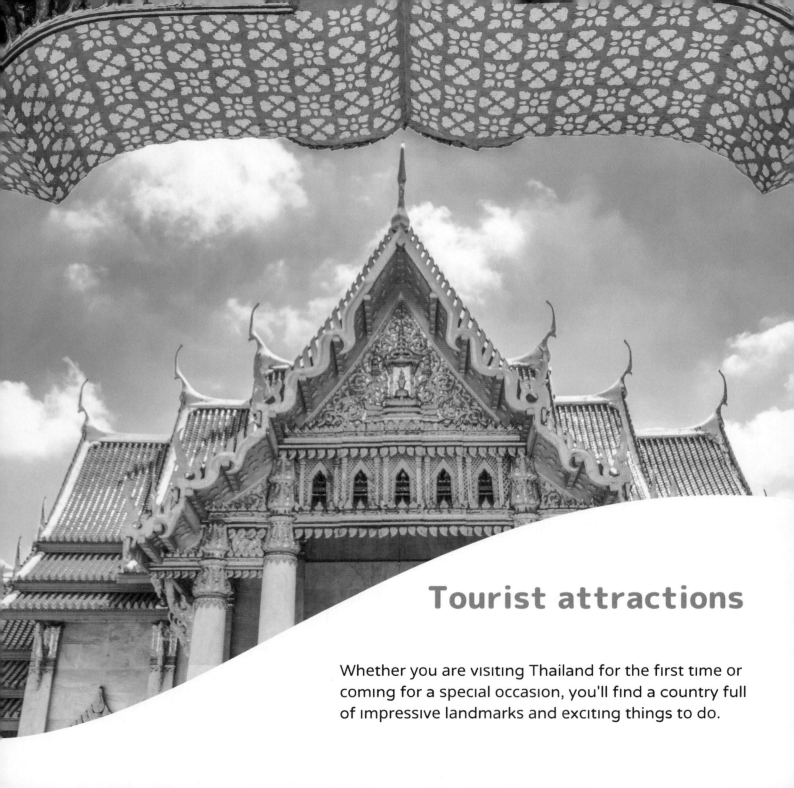

Tourist attractions

Whether you are visiting Thailand for the first time or coming for a special occasion, you'll find a country full of impressive landmarks and exciting things to do.

Ko Phi Phi

Ko Phi Phi is located in the Krabi province and it's a beautiful group of islands. The Ko Phi Phi Don is the only island within the group with permanent residents, while smaller islands are used as filming locations. Tourists go there to enjoy beaches and activities such as Scuba diving, Kayaking, and Snorkeling.

Railay Beach

Railay Beach is one of the most beautiful in Thailand. It offers white sand, turquoise-blue water, and a beautiful view. You can reach there by boat from Krabi town and Ao Nang to experience the beautiful beach and activities such as rock-climbing, kayaking, ocean rafting, and scuba diving.

Phuket

Phuket is the largest highland in Thailand. It accommodates tourists and travelers every year who come to see its golden beaches, offshore islands, upbeat markets, and nightlife experience.

Doi Inthanon

Doi Inthanon is a mountain that stands at 8,415 feet above sea level, making it the highest peak in the country. The summit of the mountain houses the ashes of the lake king Inthanon.

Floating Markets

Visiting the floating markets means you'll witness the locals' lifestyle, culture, and way of life in a single experience. You'll experience local food and souvenirs and interact with the locals. Bangkok is the most popular place for floating markets

The Grand Palace

Bangkok has many places to visit, and the Grand Palace ranks high. It's the number 1 tourist attraction because of its historical importance and value. You'll see royal halls, ancient buildings, and temples when you get there.

THAILAND FUN FACTS

The smallest and largest creatures in the world live in Thailand. Bumblebee and the Whale shark.

Festivals

Because of the large population of Chinese people, the Chinese new year is one of the largest festivals in Thailand. There are a lot of celebrations, including dragon dances, firecrackers, parades, and food. Below are some other popular festivals in Thailand.

Popular annual events and festivals

Phi Ta Khon(Ghost festival)- 3 days festival in Dan Sai Town that originated from a mixture of Buddist and animist beliefs. It combines religious traditions, fun parties, and local Handicrafts.

Songkran(Water Festival)- 3 days water fight festival in April throughout the country. It's the biggest and most fun festival in Thailand.

Yi Peng(Lantern Festival)- November festival where paper lanterns are released into the sky to float. It's relaxing and a great sight for photography.

Lopburi Monkey Banquet (Food Festival)- food festival to feed about 3000 monkeys in Lopburi in the north of Bangkok.

THAILAND FUN FACTS

Thailand has about 35,000 temples.

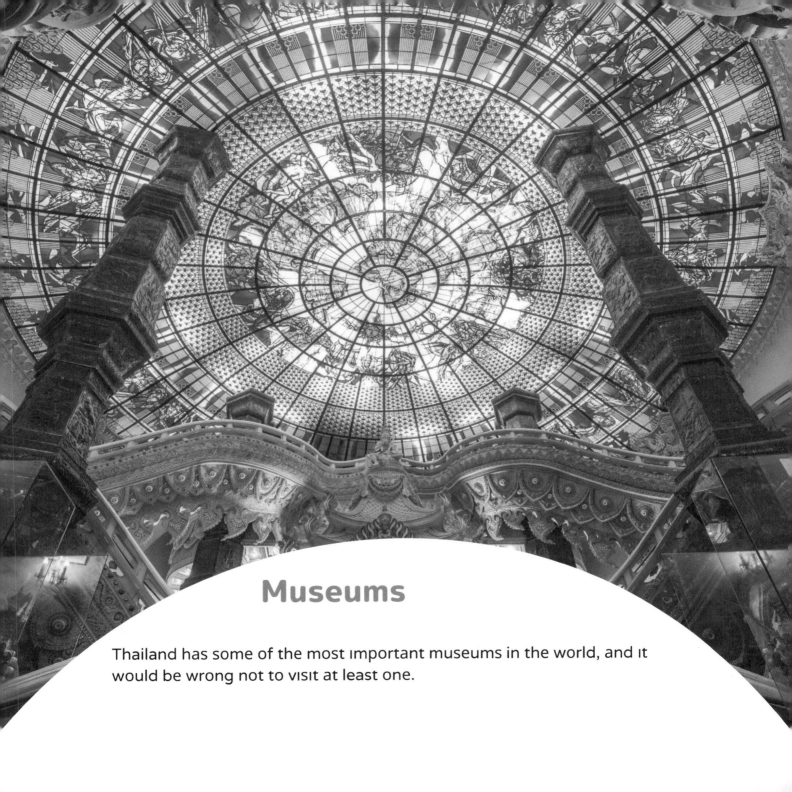

Museums

Thailand has some of the most important museums in the world, and it would be wrong not to visit at least one.

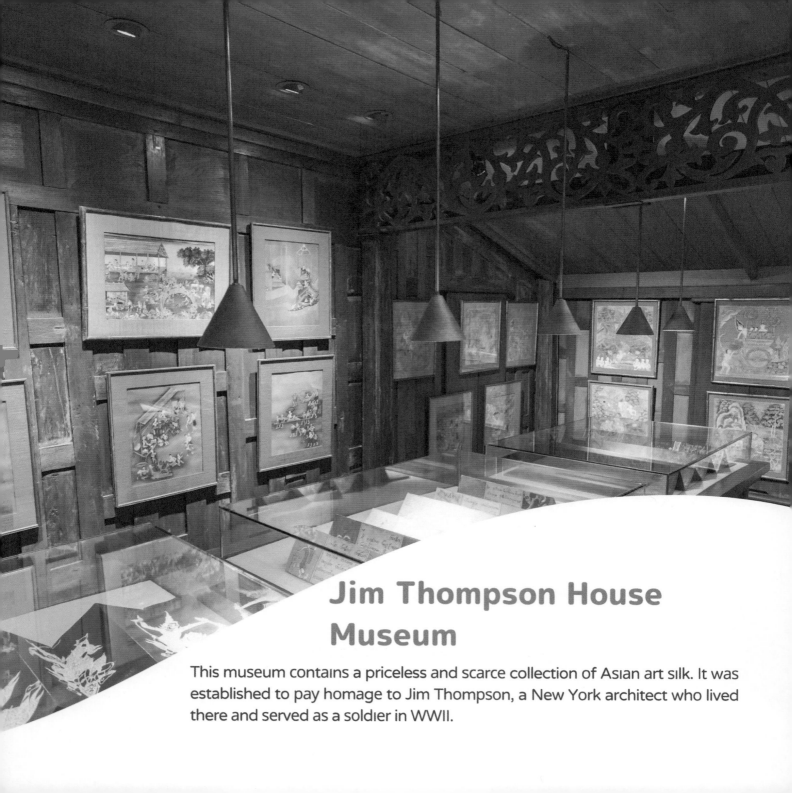

Jim Thompson House Museum

This museum contains a priceless and scarce collection of Asian art silk. It was established to pay homage to Jim Thompson, a New York architect who lived there and served as a soldier in WWII.

The National Museum Bangkok

The Museum comprises arts, royal barges, furniture, and artifacts that were passed down Thailand's history. The Museum is divided according to the type of artifact, and each building tells a Thai history.

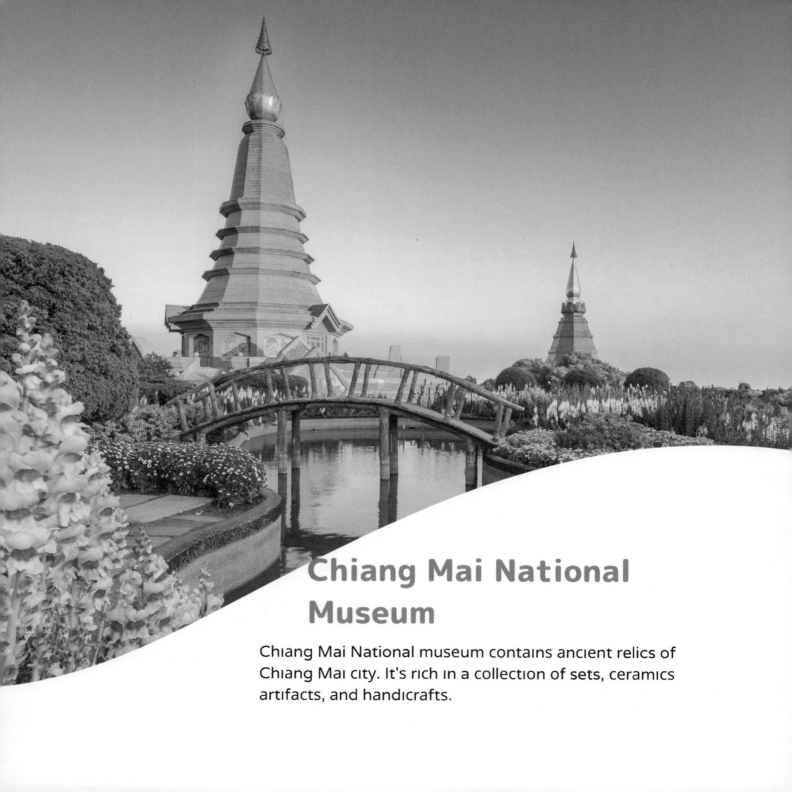

Chiang Mai National Museum

Chiang Mai National museum contains ancient relics of Chiang Mai city. It's rich in a collection of sets, ceramics artifacts, and handicrafts.

Thai-Burma Railway Centre Museum

Thai-Burma railway museum exhibits the rich history of the Burma railway, over 140km of train track that cut across Bang Pong and Thanbyuzayat during WWII.

Food and Dining

Chinese and Indian cultures influenced Thai food. Rice is standard in every meal, and most Thai foods are spicy. Common ones include basil, hot chilies, ginger, coconut milk, lemongrass, Thai curries, Tom Yum Soup, Pad Thai noodles, Som Tam Salad, and Satay.

Generally, Traditional Thai food falls into four groups: yam(spicy salads), tom(boiled food), gang(curries), and tam(pounded foods). The key to cooking Thai food revolves around balancing five important flavors- bitter, salty, sour, spicy, and sweet.

THAILAND FUN FACTS

Rice is a vital part of every meal in Thailand.

Accommodation

There's something for everyone in terms of accommodation in Thailand. Each region offers wide accommodation options. Whether low budget or expensive accommodation, private or shared, romantic getaway, and the likes, you'll find one in Thailand. Popular accommodation options include Guesthouses, hostels, bungalows, homestays, camping, national parks, and budget hotels.

Transportation

The options for transportation are numerous. From trains to buses and taxis you are faced with quality options to travel around the country. Here are transportation options in Thailand.

Songthaews and Buses

They operate inside and outside the suburbs of big cities. They are available every time, even at night. Prices differ with the type of buses, but they are not expensive.

Metered Taxi

Metered taxis are comfortable and affordable ways of traveling around Thailand. You'll see them in different colors like yellow, pink and green. The meter will show you the price of your destination, so make sure it's on when you enter. z

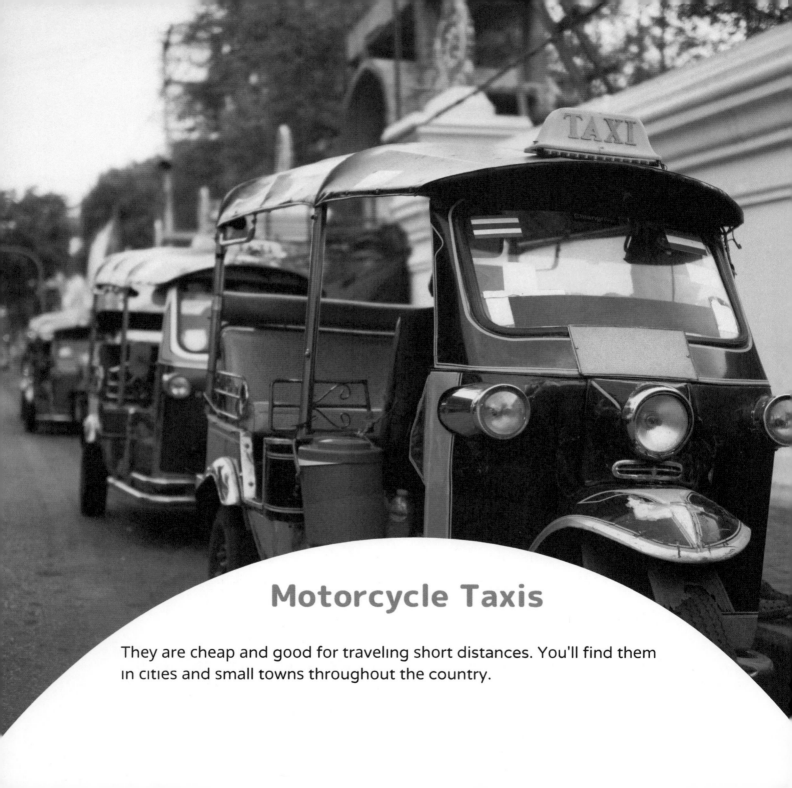

Motorcycle Taxis

They are cheap and good for traveling short distances. You'll find them in cities and small towns throughout the country.

Light Rail System

Thailand has 3 types of rail systems, so you don't have to worry about transportation. They connect major cities and are most common in Bangkok

Tuk Tuk

Tuk Tuk is similar to taxis in Thailand. Tuk Tuk is a 3-wheeled vehicle, and they are popular among tourists. But, they are more expensive than motorcycle taxis and buses.

Water buses

They are good means of transportation on Islands and big cities like Bangkok. Some provide services on Bangkok canals and work along the Chao Phraya river.

Shopping

Thailand is a great shopping destination for everything ranging from traditional Thai products to antiques and silk products to amazing ornaments. You can go for high-market names and get great bargains. Fancy malls, bazaars, night markets, floating bazaars, and stores are shopping options in Thailand. Products you can buy include Thai Silk, ceramics and pottery, furniture and earnings, Handmade Thai jewelry, Thai Loincloth, Muay, Tuk Tuk, and Wickerwork.

When to Visit Thailand?

The best time to visit Thailand is between November and April(cool and dry season) because the weather and climate are pleasant. But, the climate varies thought-out the country, so you can visit any time of the year.

Wat Arun Temple,
Bangkok, Thailand

Printed in Great Britain
by Amazon

82786870R00025